DELAWARE

DELAWARE

HELLO U.S.A.

by Dottie Brown

Lerner Publications Company

You'll find this picture of peach blossoms at the beginning of each chapter. The peach blossom is Delaware's state flower. Peaches were an important crop in Delaware in the 1800s. Then, in the late 1800s, a disease called peach yellows wiped out most of the state's peach trees. The state flower is a reminder of the peach's role in Delaware history.

Cover (left): Cultivated fields at the Winterthur estate in Delaware's Brandywine Valley. Cover (right): Sailboats in Lewes, Delaware. Pages 2–3: Breakwater Lighthouse at Delaware Bay. Page 3: Baskets of apples from T. S. Smith & Sons farm in Bridgeville, Delaware.

This book is available in two editions:
Library binding by Lerner Publications Company, a division of Lerner Publishing Group
Soft cover by First Avenue Editions, an imprint of Lerner Publishing Group
241 First Avenue North
Minneapolis, MN 55401 U.S.A.

Website address: www.lernerbooks.com

Library of Congress Cataloging-in-Publication Data

Brown, Dottie, 1957–
    Delaware / by Dottie Brown. (Rev. and expanded 2nd ed.)
        p.   cm. — (Hello U.S.A.)
    Includes index.
    Summary: Introduces the geography, history, economy, environmental issues, and people of Delaware.
    ISBN: 0–8225–4079–7 (lib. bdg. : alk. paper)
    ISBN: 0–8225–0775–7 (pbk. : alk. paper)
    1. Delaware—Juvenile literature. [1. Delaware.] I. Title. II. Series.
F164.3 .B76 2002
975.1—dc21   2001006409

Manufactured in the United States of America
1 2 3 4 5 6 – JR – 07 06 05 04 03 02

CONTENTS

The sun sets over wild grasses at Delaware Bay, Delaware.

THE LAND

Small Wonder

Blown off course, British sea captain Samuel Argall sought shelter in a bay off the Atlantic Ocean in 1610. Argall named the bay De La Warr, after the governor of Virginia. Common use shortened the name to Delaware. Soon, Europeans gave the name to the river that feeds the bay and to the Indians who already lived in the area. Later Delaware also became the name of a Mid-Atlantic state—the second smallest state in the United States.

Pennsylvania borders Delaware to the north, and Maryland forms the state's southern and western boundaries. The Delaware River, Delaware Bay, and the Atlantic Ocean shape the eastern edge of the state. Across the wide Delaware Bay lies New Jersey.

DELAWARE
Political Map

★ State capital

0   5   10 Miles

0   5   10   15   20 Kilometers

Winterthur

Wilmington

Newark

Delaware City

Smyrna

Bombay Hook
National Wildlife Refuge

Dover ★

Harrington

• Milford

Lewes •   *Cape Henlopen*
                      State Park

Rehoboth Beach •

Seaford

Oak Orchard

Millsboro

Laurel   *Trap Pond*   Ocean View
                State Park

The drawing of Delaware on this page is called a political map. It shows features created by people, including cities, railways, and parks. The map on the facing page is called a physical map. It shows physical features of Delaware, such as coasts, islands, mountains, rivers, and lakes. The colors represent a range of elevations, or heights above sea level (see legend box). This map also shows the geographical regions of Delaware.

8

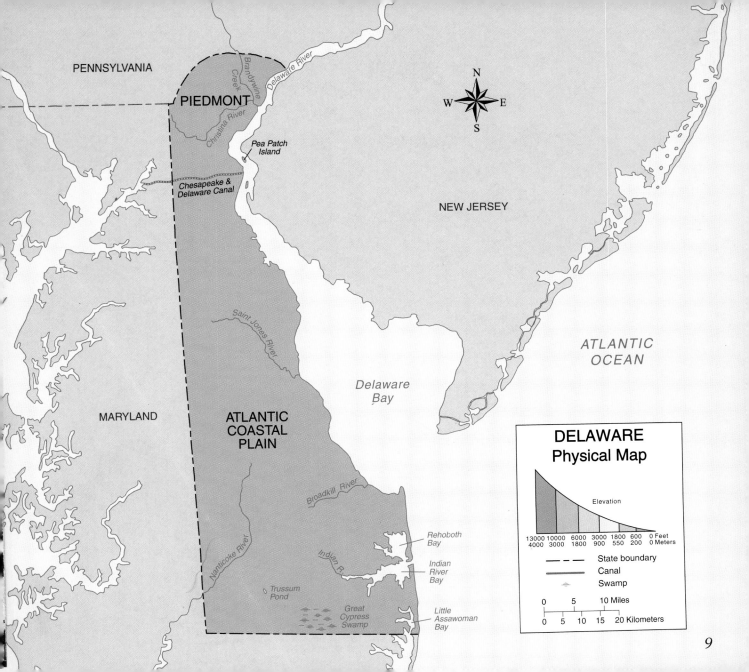

PENNSYLVANIA

PIEDMONT

Brandywine Creek

Delaware River

Christina River

Pea Patch Island

Chesapeake & Delaware Canal

NEW JERSEY

N
W E
S

MARYLAND

ATLANTIC COASTAL PLAIN

Saint Jones River

Delaware Bay

ATLANTIC OCEAN

Broadkill River

Nanticoke River

Indian R.

Rehoboth Bay

Indian River Bay

Trussum Pond

Great Cypress Swamp

Little Assawoman Bay

DELAWARE
Physical Map

Elevation

| 13000 | 10000 | 6000 | 3000 | 1800 | 600 | 0 Feet |
| 4000 | 3000 | 1800 | 900 | 550 | 200 | 0 Meters |

- - - State boundary

──── Canal

Swamp

0   5   10 Miles

0   5   10   15   20 Kilometers

9

Green algae coats the
surface of Trussum Pond
in southern Delaware.

Delaware has two major land regions. The Atlantic Coastal Plain covers almost all of the state. A small semi-circle of land called the Piedmont caps the northern tip of the coastal plain.

The soil of the low, flat Atlantic Coastal Plain is sandy. **Marshes** (grassy wetlands) line much of the shore. The Great Cypress Swamp sprawls along Delaware's southern border. This **swamp** (wooded wetland) once covered nearly five times the area it does in modern times. Farmers drained most of it to create some of the state's richest cropland.

North of the coastal plain, hilly farmland blankets much of the Piedmont. A thin layer of clay soil coats the thick, hard rock that lies underneath. Although the Piedmont stretches only 10 miles at its widest point, it is home to roughly two out of three Delawareans. Most of these people live in or near Wilmington, the state's largest city.

In spring, flowers and fruit trees blossom in the Piedmont.

Delaware has many rivers. Its largest and most important river, the Delaware, flows southward into Delaware Bay. Other chief waterways include the Christina River and Brandywine Creek, both of which empty into the Delaware River. The Broadkill, Indian, and Saint Jones Rivers cross southeastern Delaware, flowing into Delaware Bay. In southern Delaware, the Nanticoke River travels westward into Maryland.

Chilly weather doesn't keep canoeists away from the Delaware River.

Ships from around the world sail into Delaware Bay, heading for inland markets along the Delaware River. Three small bays—Rehoboth, Indian River, and Little Assawoman—lie behind long sandbars (ridges of built-up sand) in southern Delaware. The sandbars have become some of Delaware's most popular beaches.

These beaches—and the sandy soil of the Atlantic Coastal Plain—provide clues to the history of the state's land. For millions of years, most of Delaware lay deep beneath the waters of the Atlantic Ocean. Porpoises, hammerhead sharks, foot-long oysters, and other sea creatures were among the region's few living beings. Gradually, the water retreated from the land, leaving behind layers of dirt, sand, clay, gravel, and other tiny pieces of rock.

The Atlantic Ocean still affects Delaware. Hurricanes and other severe ocean storms occasionally strike Delaware's coast. Powerful winds rip apart homes, uproot trees, and blast sand off the beaches. The winds also whip the ocean into giant waves that flood the coast.

Delicate fossils of sea creatures remind Delawareans that the Atlantic Ocean once covered the state.

But most of the year, Delaware's weather is mild. Summer temperatures average 76° F and winter temperatures hover around 35° F. **Precipitation** (rain and melted snow) is plentiful in the state, averaging 45 inches a year. Although winters are fairly warm, Delaware still gets about 16 inches of snow each year. Most of the snow falls in the north.

Because of Delaware's warm climate, many different kinds of plants thrive in the state. Stands of hickory, holly, oak, pine, and beech trees cover about one-third of the state. Cypress and red cedar trees tower above Delaware's swamps, where rare orchids also bloom. Many flowering trees and bushes, including fragrant magnolias, wild cherries, and tulip trees, blossom throughout the state. Water lilies float lazily on ponds and lakes.

Lots of different animals make their homes in Delaware. Deer and mink scamper through the forests. Otters glide through the state's many streams and rivers, while muskrats creep along the swamps. Wading birds such as herons and ibis nest in wetlands along Delaware Bay. On the seacoast, crabs, clams, and oysters hide in the sand.

Tulip tree *(above)*
White-tailed deer *(left)*

A Lenape Indian legend tells that the world was built on the back of a giant turtle. Trees that grew on the turtle's back sprouted into people.

THE HISTORY

The First State

n 1967 a real-life detective story unfolded in a field along Delaware's coast. Scientists there dug up an ancient burial site that held 90 graves. With clues from stones, bones, shells, and pieces of pottery, the scientists worked to solve the puzzle about who was buried there. They discovered that the graves belonged to American Indians, or Native Americans, who had lived in the area between 1,000 and 1,500 years ago.

These Indians were among the first known people in the area that would later be named Delaware. They hunted deer, elks, beavers, and foxes for food.

They fished, and they dug clams and oysters from the seashore. The Indians also gathered seashells to decorate clothing. Prized for their beauty, some of the shells were traded to other Indians as far away as the Mississippi River.

No one knows for sure what happened to Delaware's first people. They were gone by the time European explorers arrived in the area in the 1600s. By then a different nation, or tribe, called the Lenape was living near the Delaware River and its bay.

The Lenape, whom the Europeans called the Delaware, were a peaceful people. Like the Nanticoke, their neighbors at the southern end of Delaware Bay, the Lenape lived along rivers and streams in villages of 50 to 200 people. On the outskirts of the villages, the Indians grew corn, squash, and beans. Beyond the crops were hunting grounds.

Each Indian family lived in its own dome-shaped wigwam, which was built with tree limbs, bark, and grass. The women wove baskets, sewed clothing from animal skins, and cooked meals. The men

A Lenape Indian leader speaks to his people.

fished and carved dugout
canoes to travel by water.
They also hunted deer, beavers, and other animals.
Twice a year, the entire village journeyed inland
to hunt. As they walked, the men were ready to
defend their families from danger. The women carried the belongings. Sometimes when the villagers
reached a thick grove of trees and shrubs, they set it
on fire to drive out animals for easier hunting.

The Lenape set fences across streams to keep fish from swimming away. Nets and spears helped the Lenape catch the trapped fish. The catch was then smoke-dried and stored for winter.

Though the Lenape were peaceful, the powerful Susquehannocks frequently attacked them. The Susquehannocks, who lived to the north and west, killed so many Lenape that many of the survivors fled their homelands. The Susquehannocks also attacked the Nanticoke.

Meanwhile, another threat to the Indians arrived. In 1609 explorer Henry Hudson sailed into Delaware Bay while looking for a route to Asia. Hudson quickly realized he was heading the wrong way and sailed back out the next day. But his short visit was the first of many European voyages to the area. The Europeans would change the Indians' way of life forever.

In the 1600s, many explorers came to the land that was later called the United States.

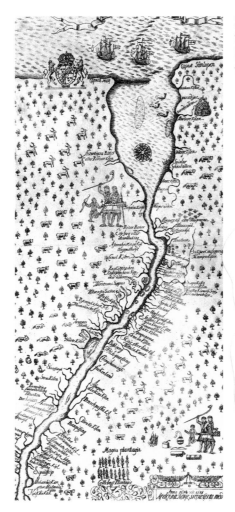

Swedes—who named the area New Sweden—built settlements along the Delaware River.

Hudson worked for the Dutch government, which soon claimed the land around the Delaware River and built a **colony,** or settlement, called Zwaanendael. The Dutch traded European goods for furs with the Lenape and made money by selling the furs in Europe.

In 1638 Swedish settlers bought land from the Lenape and built Fort Christina in what would become northern Delaware. The Swedes had heard that the area had rich farmland and good fishing. Like the Dutch, the Swedes came to make money.

Misunderstanding at Zwaanendael

In 1631 a group of about 30 Dutch people landed at what would later become Lewes, Delaware *(below right)*. So many swans swam in the marshes there that the Dutch named the area Zwaanendael, or Valley of Swans. Zwaanendael was the first colony in Delaware.

The newcomers quickly constructed some brick buildings and began to clear land for planting crops. The settlers made friends with the local Lenape, and they traded food and drink with each other. The two groups got along well until a misunderstanding arose over a painted shield of tin *(above)* hanging outside the Dutch fort.

To the Dutch, the shield was a coat of arms, a symbol of their country that commanded honor and respect. To the Lenape, it was simply an object they had never seen before.

One of the Indians took the Dutch coat of arms. The Dutch got very angry. Before long, the Indian who had taken the metal shield was found dead. One version of the story says the Dutch killed the Indian. Another account claims the Lenape killed him to keep peace with the Dutch. Either way, the Lenape later decided to get even for the death of their friend by killing all of the Dutch colonists in Zwaanendael.

The Swedes' fort stood on a river they named the Christina in honor of their country's 12-year-old queen. Inside the fort's sturdy walls, the Swedes built the first log cabins in North America. The settlers quickly went to work planting rye, pumpkins, cucumbers, turnips, and watermelons. By the 1650s, nearly 400 settlers lived in New Sweden, the first permanent European settlement in Delaware.

The Dutch worried that the Swedes might try to make money in the fur trade, too. So the Dutch sent warships up the Christina River and claimed New Sweden.

But the Dutch soon lost New Sweden to another European power, the British. In 1681 William Penn founded the large British colony of Pennsylvania to the north. Penn needed a route to the sea, so he took control of coastal lands in the region known as Delaware.

Penn divided Delaware into three counties—New Castle, Kent, and Sussex. Together they became known as the Three Lower Counties because they were south of Pennsylvania. As the

When the Three Lower Counties were part of Pennsylvania, colonists there had their own paper money.

colony's governor, Penn allowed the Three Lower Counties to make their own laws, which gave the colonists a great deal of freedom.

North of the Three Lower Counties, Philadelphia quickly became an important center of trade and the fastest growing town in Pennsylvania. Farms sprang up along the rivers and streams of New Castle because it was closer to Philadelphia than Kent and Sussex were. Farmers shipped wheat, rye, barley, and corn up the Delaware River to be sold in Philadelphia.

The process of grinding grain into flour required many machines, as this model of a flour mill shows.

Wilmington, in New Castle County, became a thriving town on Brandywine Creek. The stream's swiftly flowing water was used to power mills that ground wheat into flour. Flour from the Brandywine mills was famous for how white and finely ground it was.

As more and more Europeans moved into the Three Lower Counties, the Native Americans of the region lost land they had depended on for hunting and farming. Also, many Indians died from diseases they caught from the Europeans. To escape these problems, the Lenape kept moving farther west. By the mid-1700s, all the Lenape had left the Three Lower Counties. Many Nanticoke also had left.

At about the same time, Great Britain was at war with France, fighting for control of the North American fur trade. The British wanted the colonists in Pennsylvania and other North American colonies to help pay for the war. So the British government passed a series of laws forcing the colonists to pay taxes on tea, glass, paper, and other items that came from Britain.

A statue in Wilmington honors Caesar Rodney, a representative to the colonial government from the Three Lower Counties. Like many colonists, Rodney didn't like the new taxes passed by Britain.

Troops from Delaware march off to fight in the American Revolution.

The colonists were angry about the taxes. Many colonists decided they wanted to be free of British rule. By 1776 all 13 British colonies in North America had joined together to fight a war—called the American Revolution—to gain independence from Britain.

After the Three Lower Counties entered the war, they separated from Pennsylvania and united to form the state of Delaware. British troops occupied Delaware for several weeks in 1777 and controlled the Delaware River for eight months.

Many Delawareans fought in the Revolution, helping the colonies win independence from Britain in 1783. Four years later, Delaware became the first state to approve the **constitution** (basic written laws) of the United States—the country formed by the former colonists. For this reason, Delawareans earned the nickname First Staters.

After the war, many businesses thrived in Delaware. Shipyards were built in nearly all the port towns along Delaware's rivers. Shipbuilders crafted wooden sloops, schooners, and fishing boats out of pine and white oak. Paper mills and cloth mills also prospered, and Wilmington continued to grow as a center for flour milling.

Boats called sloops were sailing up Brandywine Creek by 1830. The sloops delivered wheat from surrounding states and then carried flour to Philadelphia and beyond.

Soon the Brandywine Creek's strong current attracted a new kind of miller. In 1801 a wealthy French **immigrant** named Éleuthère Irénée du Pont bought a large stretch of land north of Wilmington. Having learned how to make fine gunpowder in France, du Pont built large powder mills along the Brandywine in 1802. The mills quickly became successful.

At the same time, new crushed-gravel roads called **turnpikes** gave farmers in northern Delaware an easier route to markets. Farmers could sell more wool, butter, and other products.

Delaware's lawmakers meet in Dover's Legislative Hall, which is patterned after government buildings from the late 1700s.

Some of Delaware's farmers owned slaves from Africa, but most of the black people in the state were free. Many Delawareans and people in other Northern states wanted to end slavery entirely.

Travel by boat improved after steamboats were built in the early 1800s. Ships no longer had to rely on wind to move them through the water. Paddling along Delaware's rivers, steamboats carried passengers, coal, lumber, and gravel in record time.

Steamboats rely on steam power and a paddle to move.

A State Divided

The people of Delaware could not agree on whether slavery was right or wrong. The state had some laws that helped African Americans. Other laws worked against them. Slavery was allowed, but the state passed a law forbidding any new slaves from being brought into Delaware. African Americans were considered free unless they were proven to be slaves, but, like slaves, free blacks were not permitted to enter the state.

Two famous Delawareans, Patty Cannon (right) and Thomas Garrett (above), held two very different opinions about slavery. Cannon led a gang that kidnapped slaves and free blacks and sold them to slave traders. Sometimes Cannon even murdered the slave traders in order to take all of their money. Kidnapping was illegal, but it was murder that finally got Cannon arrested. She died in jail, waiting to be hanged.

Thomas Garrett, however, believed slavery was wrong and devoted his life to helping slaves reach freedom. While living in Delaware, he helped about 3,000 escaped slaves reach Pennsylvania, where slavery was not allowed.

Helping slaves escape was illegal in Delaware, and eventually Garrett was caught. The judge who heard his case gave him a big fine, and Garrett lost all his property in order to pay it. But the heavy penalty did not stop Garrett. He told the judge that he would still help any slave who came his way.

In 1829 the Chesapeake and Delaware Canal was completed. This water route linked towns along Delaware Bay to important markets on the Chesapeake Bay in Maryland. The canal cut hundreds of miles off the route between the two bays.

The Chesapeake and Delaware Canal sped up shipping between Maryland and Delaware.

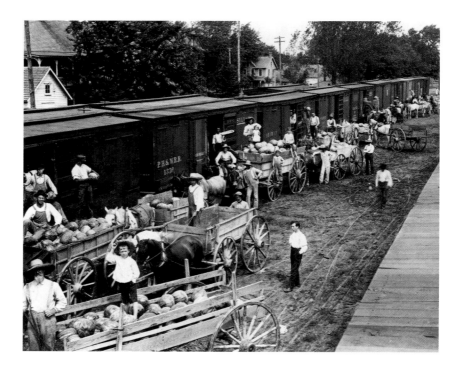

Produce such as watermelons can be carried much more quickly by train than by wagon. In the 1800s, farmers began to use railroads to distribute their fruits and vegetables.

In the 1830s, Delawareans began laying railroad tracks. The railroads reached into Kent and Sussex Counties. For the first time, farmers in southern Delaware had an easy way to get their crops to market. New towns sprang up all along the tracks. Some Delawarean farmers still used slave labor, but many did not. Most people in the Northern United States opposed slavery.

Southern states depended on unpaid slave labor to earn a profit on **plantations,** or large farms. When Northern states tried to force Southerners to end slavery, several Southern states formed their own country, the Confederate States of America, in 1861.

Soon after, the Civil War broke out between the North and the South. Delaware joined the Union, or Northern, forces. Most of the state's soldiers fought for the Union. But some Delawareans sided with the South.

After the Civil War, African Americans who were previously slaves became free.

The fortress of Fort Delaware, which was used during the Civil War, still stands.

Du Pont's mills provided more than one-third of the Union's gunpowder. Fort Delaware, on Pea Patch Island in the Delaware River, held Confederate prisoners of war.

After the Union won the war in 1865, slaves throughout the South were freed, and black men gained the right to vote. But white Delawareans worried about the power African Americans might have if they voted. The state passed a law requiring people to pay a tax before they could vote. Many black men couldn't afford to pay the tax, and tax collectors refused to take money from those who could.

New inventions spurred the growth of industry in the years following the Civil War. In northern Delaware, where most of the state's industry was centered, trains brought in coal and iron ore from Pennsylvania to make steel. Wilmington's factories used the steel to make transportation equipment. Delaware became one of the biggest manufacturers of trolley cars, train cars, and riverboats.

Several large ironworks in Delaware, such as the Pusey & Jones Company, turned out ships and other iron products.

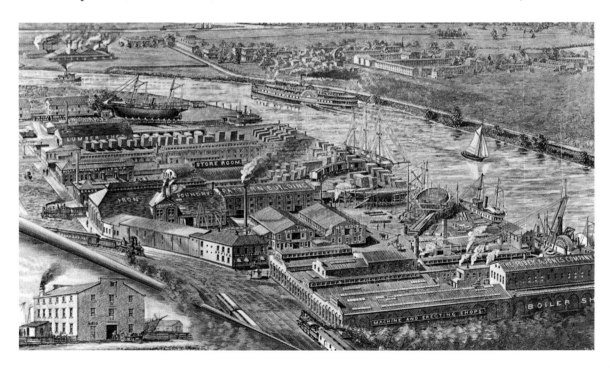

Alfred

Coleman

Pierre

The du Ponts

When three young du Pont cousins— Coleman, Alfred, and Pierre—became the Du Pont Company's leaders in 1902, the men quickly turned the Delaware business into one of the largest in the United States. But the family that ran the company was important in other ways, too.

In 1910 Coleman du Pont gave Delaware $4 million to build the nation's first divided highway. The new roadway boosted the state's economy by providing farms and factories with a fast and easy route to get products to market.

Alfred du Pont took a strong interest in children and in the elderly. In 1929 he started a plan to give money to old people who could no longer work for a living. And upon his death, Alfred donated much of his fortune to set up an institute for disabled children.

Throughout the early 1900s, Pierre du Pont paid for many new schools for African Americans. He also set up educational standards that all schools had to meet. The large sums of money Pierre donated greatly improved education in the state for both white and African American students.

The state's tanneries made expensive leather from animal skins. Mining and construction companies throughout the country bought gunpowder milled in Delaware. The companies needed the gunpowder to blast away layers of rock that covered minerals and to clear paths for building roads.

During World War I (1914–1918), Delaware's shipyards bustled to build ships for the fighting overseas. Gunpowder companies worked day and night. After the war, these companies branched into new areas as their chemists developed dyes, paints, and chemically produced fabrics such as rayon. They also developed plastic.

The outbreak of World War II (1939–1945) also boosted Delaware's economy. After the war, some large companies chose to move to Delaware because laws in the state were friendly to businesses. Delaware's population increased dramatically as these big companies brought many of their workers with them.

During World War II, a worker in the plastics department at Du Pont assembles the nose of a bomber plane.

The new companies also made more jobs available for white Delawareans. But African Americans did not have as many choices. They could not attend the same schools as white students or go to the same restaurants and theaters. In 1952 Delaware ruled that the separation of black people and white people in public places was against the law.

White communities were very slow to accept the ruling. Poor housing for black people was one of many issues that led to riots in Wilmington in 1967 and 1968. Delaware's governor called in the National Guard to end the violence.

After the riots, the state passed a fair-housing law to make sure African Americans had the same chances as white people to live in decent housing. The state also passed laws to ensure that black students were allowed to attend the same schools as white students. And in 1968, James Sills became the first African American elected to serve on Wilmington's city council.

During the 1980s and 1990s, business in Delaware grew. Big companies, especially banks, moved to

In the 1960s, laws were passed in Delaware to ensure equality for all its citizens.

the state because of its low taxes and laws that made it easy to open and run businesses. The state's population increased as the economy boomed.

In the early 2000s, Delawareans are trying to improve their state's schools, keep the environment clean, and make sure their state is a healthy, safe place. In 2001 Ruth Ann Minner became the First State's first woman governor.

First Staters know they have accomplished a lot, and they are willing to work hard to achieve more. As a former governor of Delaware once said, "The state that started a nation can also lead a nation."

Built in 1910, the Nemours Mansion and Gardens near Wilmington are patterned after a French estate of the 1600s.

PEOPLE & ECONOMY

Beaches and Businesses

drive across the longest part of Delaware takes less than three hours, and a trip across the widest part takes less than one. Delaware is the second smallest state in the nation. And with only about 784,000 people, it has the sixth smallest population in the United States.

Delaware may not be a large state, but it can boast about how much it packs into a small area. For instance, the Nemours Mansion and Gardens is only a short drive from Wilmington. There, visitors can tour Alfred du Pont's French country estate, complete with a château (castle) and formal gardens.

Du Pont's background was French, but many Delawareans are descendants of the state's early Swedish, Dutch, and British colonists. African Americans make up about 19 percent of the state's population. A small number of Indians who are descendants of the Nanticoke still live in Delaware. Asian Americans make up about 2 percent of Delawareans. **Latinos,** or people with Latin American ancestry, make up about 5 percent of the population.

Three-fourths of all Delawareans live in cities, or **urban** areas. Wilmington is Delaware's biggest urban area. The state capital, Dover, is in central Delaware and ranks as the second largest city. On the state's northwestern border lies Newark, Delaware's third largest city.

Swedish settlers built the Old Swedes Church in Wilmington more than 300 years ago.

A descendant of the Nanticoke Indians performs a traditional dance in Delaware.

Delaware's cities offer many opportunities, including the chance to find out what life was like in another time. At Winterthur Museum, people can stroll through more than 100 rooms that display American art and furniture dating as far back as 1640. In Dover, visitors can stand on the very spot where Delawareans voted to approve the U.S. Constitution in 1787, making Delaware the first state.

Throughout the year, festivals draw visitors to Delaware's cities and state parks. Each May on Old Dover Day, many historic homes and buildings in the capital city are open to the public in a celebration of the state's heritage.

A doll's tea party from the 1800s is on display *(above)* at the Winterthur Museum. Historic buildings and cobblestone streets can be found throughout Delaware. The state's first capital city was New Castle *(right)*.

Wind fills the sails of these sailboats on Rehoboth Bay.

That same month, Milford hosts the World Champion Weakfish Tournament, where First Staters try to catch a fish whose mouth is so weak that lifting it from the water by a hook will tear it. In the fall, the Nanticoke Indians hold a two-day powwow in Millsboro, where they perform ceremonial dances, tell stories, and demonstrate Indian crafts.

Throughout the summer months, sun and surf lovers flock to southern Delaware's Rehoboth Beach, one of the state's most popular recreation sites. The beach has even been nicknamed the Nation's Summer Capital because so many visitors come from Washington, D.C. The nation's capital city, Washington, D.C., is about 125 miles west of Rehoboth Beach.

At the Winterthur Point-to-Point Races, jockeys race to the finish line.

Outdoor enthusiasts also can hike in Delaware's state parks, bike from inn to inn along the seashore, or try their luck at catching tuna, shark, and marlin in the Atlantic Ocean. And the excitement of squealing tires and fast cars lures fans to Dover Downs International Speedway.

When First Staters are not playing, they work in a variety of jobs. Many of Delaware's workers provide services such as selling homes, repairing automobiles, and flying airplanes. Other types of service jobs include waiting tables, selling clothing, and driving trucks. More Delawareans have service jobs than any other type of work.

About one-fifth of the money Delaware earns comes from manufacturing goods. Chemical products such as medicines, plastics, paints, nylon, and special materials used for space travel are among the most important items First Staters make. The state also ranks as one of the nation's leading automakers.

Shipping is an important service industry for this coastal state.

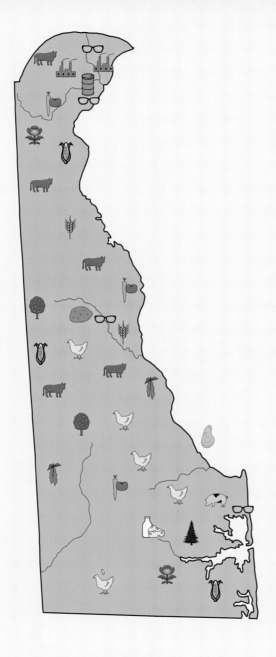

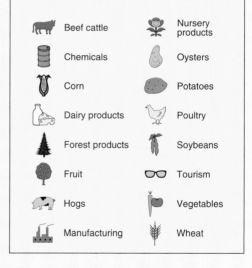

DELAWARE
Economic Map

The symbols on this map show where different economic activities take place in Delaware. The legend below explains what each symbol stands for.

	Beef cattle		Nursery products
	Chemicals		Oysters
	Corn		Potatoes
	Dairy products		Poultry
	Forest products		Soybeans
	Fruit		Tourism
	Hogs		Vegetables
	Manufacturing		Wheat

Raising chickens for food is a big industry in Delaware.

Delaware's workers prepare several types of food, too. Some people cook puddings, can pickles, or make soft drinks. Others process fish or pluck and package chickens. Still others bake desserts, breads, and pastries.

Although only 2 out of every 100 Delawareans work in agriculture, farms cover about half the state. Huge poultry farms in the south raise millions of broilers, or young chickens—Delaware's most valuable farm product. The sale of broilers earns Delaware more than $500 million each year. Dairy farms, most of which are located in central and northern Delaware, produce about $25 million worth of milk each year.

Some farmers in the state grow soybeans and corn, Delaware's most important crops. Most of the soybeans and corn are used to make feed for broilers. Other big crops include barley, wheat, peas, and potatoes. Apples are the largest fruit crop.

Delawareans gather a harvest from the sea, too. Each year workers in the fishing industry catch more than $6 million worth of crabs, clams, oysters, lobsters, sea bass, and weakfish.

With so many crops and products and with so much to see and do, First Staters can boast about many things. Delaware may be a small state, but it makes a big contribution to the nation.

THE ENVIRONMENT

Sparkling Waterways

Delaware's rivers and bays have long provided transportation, food, jobs, and recreation. But these waters are in trouble. As Delaware has grown, factories, farms, and people have polluted its waterways.

With its wide opening, Delaware Bay can rely on a fresh supply of ocean water to flush out many pollutants. But to the south, three inland bays— Rehoboth, Indian River, and Little Assawoman— share only one small opening to the ocean. As a result, pollution in the three bays collects much faster than it can flow out of them. The buildup of pollution has started a chain of events that could harm much of the bays' wildlife and could close popular beaches.

A muskrat enjoys a snack along the shore.

A fisher reels in his line on Rehoboth Bay's Silver Lake.

Pollution in the inland bays is one example of **nonpoint pollution,** which can't be pinpointed to just one place. Much of the nonpoint pollution comes from southern Delaware's many farms.

For example, farmers use chemicals called pesticides to kill insect pests. Farmers also use fertilizers to help crops grow. Fertilizers contain nutrients, which help nourish plants. Sometimes manure is used as a natural fertilizer. But in addition to nutrients, manure also contains bacteria, or germs that can cause disease. When farmers apply too much fertilizer and pesticide to their fields, rain washes away the bacteria, the chemicals, and the excess nutrients. Rain also washes away loose soil.

Dead broilers from the state's poultry farms also produce bacteria. Some of the birds die of natural causes and cannot be sold for their meat, so they are buried. As the broilers decay, bacteria forms and pollutes the soil. This bacteria also gets washed away during rainstorms.

Rainwater that carries pollutants such as bacteria, chemicals, nutrients, and loose soil is called **runoff.** The runoff flows into streams that empty into the bays, where the pollutants change the natural order of life in the water.

Polluted rainwater can puddle and drain into lakes and rivers.

For example, nutrients feed rootless water plants called algae. But with so many excess nutrients from runoff, too many algae grow on the surface of the water. Eventually, the algae die. In the process, they use up oxygen that fish need to survive.

The speed of water *(above)* tells how fast pollution travels through Indian River Bay. Scientists *(right)* use a meter to monitor how fast the water is moving.

Bacteria and chemicals from the runoff are eaten by fish and other sea creatures. When they consume these pollutants, fish and shellfish become unsafe for people to eat. High levels of bacteria also can make swimmers sick.

Many Delawareans realize that nonpoint pollution is a serious problem. Farmers and state officials are working together to solve it. Before applying fertilizer to their crops, farmers can test the soil to see how much fertilizer they need to grow healthy crops. Farmers then can adjust their machines to spread just the right amount of fertilizer.

It's unsafe to harvest oysters, mussels, and clams at some Delaware beaches *(above left)*. Pollution in the inland bays endangers the lives of sea creatures such as the horseshoe crab *(above right)*.

Farmers are taking other steps to prevent runoff, too. Instead of plowing up crops after each harvest, many farmers leave crop stubble on the ground and plow through it in the spring. The plant cover helps hold the soil and nutrients in place.

To help reduce the spread of bacteria, Delaware encourages poultry farmers not to bury dead broilers. Instead, farmers can place birds in dead-bird composters. By layering straw and manure along with the dead birds, farmers can trap enough heat in a composter to make the birds decay quickly. In just a couple of months, farmers have a heap of compost, or very fertile soil, to use on their fields.

Delaware's state officials and business people are working to educate

To help control the spread of bacteria, farmers compost dead chickens in large bins.

other Delawareans about nonpoint pollution, too. For example, industries give free education kits to teachers so schoolchildren can learn about pollution and how to prevent it.

Together, Delawareans are learning how to tackle nonpoint pollution. By cooperating to reduce pollution, First Staters can ensure a clean and healthy future for their inland bays.

Delaware's shores are home to thousands of waterbirds that depend on clean water for survival.

Fun Facts

Delaware's Dover Air Force Base houses the largest cargo planes in the world. Each one is so big it could carry 48 Cadillacs or 25,844,746 Ping-Pong balls.

Delaware was the first state to join the United States of America.

So many big chemical companies have their headquarters in Wilmington, Delaware, that the city is known as the Chemical Capital of the World.

Cypress trees—common in the southern United States—can be found as far north as the Great Cypress Swamp in southern Delaware.

More bananas are shipped into the United States through Wilmington, Delaware, than through any other port in the country.

The first log cabins in North America were built in 1638 by Swedish settlers in what would become known as Delaware.

Delaware is the only state that is partly shaped like a circle. Its northern border with Pennsylvania was drawn in a perfect arc, giving Delaware its unique form.

Fighting illness and weather, Delawarean Caesar Rodney rode 80 miles to Philadelphia, Pennsylvania, in 1776 to cast his state's vote for American independence.

Banana-filled trucks leave Wilmington, Delaware, to distribute bananas throughout the country.

STATE SONG

"Our Delaware" was adopted as Delaware's official state song in 1925.

OUR DELAWARE

Words by George B. Hynson
Music by Will M. S. Brown

You can hear "Our Delaware" by visiting this website:
<http://www.50states.com/songs/delaware.htm>

A DELAWARE RECIPE

You can make Ginger Peachy Chicken with two important Delaware products—broiler chickens and peaches. Sussex County, Delaware, produces more broiler chickens than any other county in the United States. And peaches were once such an important crop in Delaware that the state flower is the peach blossom.

GINGER PEACHY CHICKEN

4 skinless, boneless chicken breasts
salt
cracked black pepper
2 tablespoons butter
1 lemon, thinly sliced by an adult
1 can (15¼ ounces) sliced cling peaches in syrup, undrained
1½ teaspoons ground ginger

1. Season chicken lightly with salt and pepper.
2. Ask an adult to help you heat butter in large nonstick skillet over medium heat.
3. Add chicken. Sauté 6 to 8 minutes on each side or until golden brown.
4. Top with unpeeled lemon slices. Add peaches with their syrup and ginger.
5. Cover skillet. Let simmer over medium heat for 10 minutes. Baste chicken with juices while it cooks. Chicken is done when it's glazed with juices and appears thoroughly cooked.

Serves 4.

HISTORICAL TIMELINE

A.D. 500–1000 American Indians are living in Delaware.

1609 Henry Hudson sails into Delaware Bay.

1631 Dutch settlers found Zwaanendael but are killed by Native Americans.

1638 Swedes build Fort Christina at what became known as Wilmington.

1681 William Penn founds Pennsylvania.

1682 Delaware—the Three Lower Counties—comes under the control of William Penn.

mid-1700s Lenape Indians leave the Three Lower Counties.

1775 The American Revolution (1775–1783) begins.

1787 Delaware becomes the first state in the United States.

1802 Éleuthère Irénée du Pont builds gunpowder mills on Brandywine Creek.

1829 The Chesapeake and Delaware Canal opens.

1861–1865 Fort Delaware holds Confederate prisoners during the Civil War (1861–1865).

1914–1918 Delaware builds warships for World War I (1914–1918).

1938 A Du Pont factory begins making nylon.

1951 The Delaware Memorial Bridge crosses the Delaware River to link Delaware to New Jersey.

1952 The separation of white people and black people in public is made illegal in Delaware.

1967 Scientists find an ancient burial site holding the graves of 90 Native Americans along Delaware's coast.

1968 The National Guard ends race riots in Wilmington.

1987 Delaware celebrates its 200th anniversary as the First State.

2001 Ruth Ann Minner becomes Delaware's first woman governor.

OUTSTANDING DELAWAREANS

Richard Allen

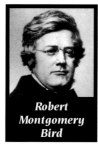

Valerie Bertinelli

Robert Montgomery Bird

Henry S. Canby

Richard Allen (1760–1831) was born into slavery and grew up on a plantation near Dover. After buying his freedom, he founded the Free African Society and the African Methodist Episcopal Church. The church became a stop for the Underground Railroad, a network of secret paths for escaped slaves heading North to freedom.

Valerie Bertinelli (born 1960) is an actress who has starred in many movies, including *Aladdin and His Wonderful Lamp*, *C.H.O.M.P.S.*, and *Shattered Vows*. In 2001 she joined the cast of the television series *Touched by an Angel*. Bertinelli is from Wilmington.

Joseph R. Biden Jr. (born 1942) has represented Delaware in the U.S. Senate since 1973. The Democrat has worked to fight the spread of drugs and crime. Biden lives in Wilmington.

Robert Montgomery Bird (1806–1854) was born in New Castle, Delaware. He began his career as a doctor but left medicine to write plays. *The Gladiator* was so popular that it was performed 1,000 times in 22 years. Bird also wrote the novel *Nick of the Woods: or, The Jippenainosay*.

Henry S. Canby (1878–1961), who taught at Yale University for more than 20 years, was a writer from Wilmington. He is perhaps best remembered as the founder and first editor of the *Saturday Review of Literature*.

Annie Jump Cannon (1863–1941) was born in Dover. Cannon was the first astronomer to prove that nearly all stars can be grouped according to colors. She discovered five new stars and classified more than 375,000 others during her lifetime.

Wallace Carothers (1896–1937) moved to Delaware in 1928 to work for the Du Pont Company, where he developed nylon. The fabric, which is made from woven fibers created in a laboratory, is very strong and has many uses.

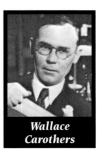

Wallace Carothers

Mary Ann Shadd Cary (1823–1893) worked to help African Americans in the United States and Canada. Born in Wilmington, she taught at schools for black children in Delaware and Pennsylvania. Cary later moved to Canada, where she became the first female African American newspaper editor in North America.

John M. Clayton (1796–1856) served numerous terms in the U.S. Senate and was secretary of state under President Zachary Taylor. Born in Dagsboro, Delaware, Clayton also served as chief justice of Delaware's supreme court.

John M. Clayton

Felix Darley (1822–1888), a popular illustrator, moved to Claymont, Delaware, in 1859. He illustrated *Rip Van Winkle, The Legend of Sleepy Hollow,* and many other works by well-known authors.

Felix Darley

George Dallas Green Jr. (born 1934) pitched for baseball's Philadelphia Phillies and New York Mets and played football with the Washington Redskins. Later, Green managed the Phillies, leading them to a 1980 World Series victory. Green is from Newport, Delaware.

Henry Jay Heimlich (born 1920), a native of Wilmington, developed the Heimlich maneuver in 1974. Within 12 years, Dr. Heimlich's simple technique, which almost anyone can use, had saved more than 10,000 people from choking to death.

George Dallas Green Jr.

John Bassett Moore

Howard Pyle

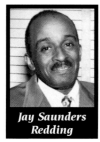

Jay Saunders Redding

Caesar Rodney

John P. Marquand (1893–1960) wrote about wealthy but misguided people living in New England. He won a Pulitzer Prize in 1938 for his novel, *The Late George Apley*. Marquand was from Wilmington.

John Bassett Moore (1860–1947), a noted lawyer born in Smyrna, Delaware, was widely respected for his view of international law. Moore was one of the first judges appointed to the World Court.

Howard Pyle (1853–1911), born in Wilmington, Delaware, painted colonial scenes and worked as an illustrator and art teacher. He wrote and illustrated many children's books, including *The Story of Jack Ballister's Fortunes*, *The Merry Adventures of Robin Hood*, and *Modern Aladdin*.

Jay Saunders Redding (1906–1988) wrote about what life was like for African Americans in *No Day of Triumph* and *On Being Black in America*. Redding also helped found the field of African American studies and taught at several of the nation's finest universities, including Hampton Institute and Cornell. Redding was a native of Washington, Delaware.

Caesar Rodney (1728–1784) was a patriot of the American Revolution and a signer of the Declaration of Independence. Rodney became a Delaware hero when he rode to Philadelphia through a thunderstorm, fighting cancer and asthma, to cast Delaware's vote for freedom. Rodney's famous ride is remembered on the 1999 Delaware quarter.

Christopher Short (born 1937), a native of Milford, Delaware, pitched for the Philadelphia Phillies from 1959 to 1972. Known as the greatest left-hander in Phillies' history, Short had four different seasons in which he won 17 or more games.

Upton Sinclair (1878–1968) was a writer whose work often dealt with social problems. He became famous after his book *The Jungle* exposed the unsafe and unclean working conditions in the meat-packing industry. Sinclair and his family lived in Arden, Delaware, for several years.

Upton Sinclair

Edward Robinson Squibb (1819–1900), a naval surgeon from Wilmington, believed medicines used by the U.S. Navy were so poor that they kept sailors from getting well. He convinced the navy to build its own drug factory. He later went on to start his own company—Squibb Pharmaceuticals.

Peter Stuyvesant (1610?–1672) was the leader of a Dutch colony in America. As governor of New Netherland (which included what became New York City) Stuyvesant overthrew the Swedish settlers living in Delaware and claimed the area for the Dutch in 1655. He was forced to surrender New Netherland to the English in 1664.

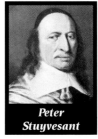
Peter Stuyvesant

Estelle Taylor (1899–1958), from Wilmington, was a star of silent movies and early sound-track films. She played leading roles in *Don Juan* and in the 1923 production of *The Ten Commandments.*

Estelle Taylor

Randy Lee White (born 1953) won All-American honors as a fullback and a linebacker at Thomas McKean High School in Wilmington. From 1975 to 1988, White played defensive tackle for the Dallas Cowboys. Known as the Monster because of his speed, strength, and fierce playing, White made a total of 1,104 tackles in his career.

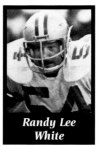
Randy Lee White

FACTS-AT-A-GLANCE

Nicknames: First State, Blue Hen State

Song: "Our Delaware"

Motto: Liberty and Independence

Flower: peach blossom

Tree: American holly

Bird: blue hen chicken

Mineral: sillimanite

Beverage: milk

Fish: weakfish

Insect: ladybug

Date and ranking of statehood:
    December 7, 1787, the first state

Capital: Dover

Area: 1,995 square miles

Rank in area, nationwide: 49th

Average January temperature: 35° F

Average July temperature: 76° F

The colors on Delaware's state flag honor George Washington. The general wore a uniform of colonial blue and buff. The state's coat of arms appears in the center of the flag.

POPULATION GROWTH

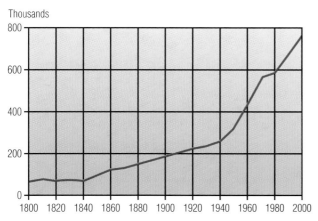

Thousands

This chart shows how Delaware's population has grown from 1800 to 2000.

Delaware's state seal was adopted in 1777. Like the state flag, Delaware's seal depicts the state coat of arms. A farmer, a soldier, and a sailing ship surround a shield. An ox, an ear of corn, and a sheaf of wheat appear on the shield. Together, these symbols stand for the First State's rich agriculture, strong shipping industry, and commitment to American freedom.

Population: 783,600 (2000 census)

Rank in population, nationwide: 45th

Major cities and populations: (2000 census) Wilmington (72,664), Dover (32,135), Newark (28,547), Milford (6,732), Seaford (6,699)

U.S. senators: 2

U.S. representatives: 1

Electoral votes: 3

Natural resources: Brandywine blue granite, magnesium, sand and gravel

Agricultural products: apples, barley, chickens, corn, flowers, hogs, milk, peas, potatoes, shrubs, soybeans, wheat

Fishing industry: carp, clams, crabs, eels, lobsters, oysters, sea bass, sea trout, shad, weakfish

Manufactured goods: canned vegetables, cars, drugs, fish products, gelatin, industrial chemicals, nylon, packaged chicken, paper products, plastics, pudding, soft drinks

WHERE DELAWAREANS WORK

Services—66 percent (services includes jobs in trade; community, social, and personal services; finance, insurance, and real estate; transportation, communication, and utilities)

Manufacturing—13 percent

Government—13 percent

Construction—6 percent

Agriculture—2 percent

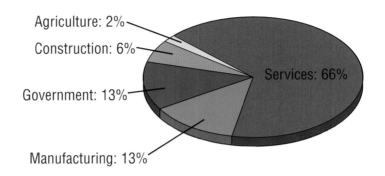

Agriculture: 2%
Construction: 6%
Government: 13%
Services: 66%
Manufacturing: 13%

GROSS STATE PRODUCT

Services—66 percent

Manufacturing—20 percent

Government—9 percent

Construction—4 percent

Agriculture—1 percent

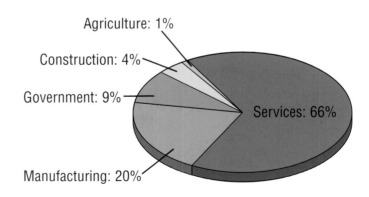

Agriculture: 1%
Construction: 4%
Government: 9%
Services: 66%
Manufacturing: 20%

STATE WILDLIFE

Mammals: deer, foxes, mink, muskrat, otter, rabbit

Birds: cardinal, ducks, hawks, herons, ibis, oriole, ruby-throated hummingbird, sandpiper, snowy egret, wrens

Amphibians and reptiles: frogs, salamander, snake, snapping turtle, toads

Fish: bass, carp, catfish, clams, crabs, eel, menhaden, oysters, shad, trout, white perch

Trees: beech, black tupelo, cypress, hickory, holly, oak, pine, red cedar, sassafras, tulip tree, willow

Wild plants: blueberry, cranberry, floating heart, hibiscus, magnolia, pink lady's-slipper, water lily, wild cherry

Blue heron

PLACES TO VISIT

Bombay Hook National Wildlife Refuge, near Smyrna
More than 15,000 acres of Delaware's seacoast make up this important waterfowl refuge. Birdwatchers can spot ducks, geese, herons, and glossy ibis.

Cape Henlopen State Park, near Lewes
Beautiful sandy beaches attract thousands of bathers each year. An observation tower provides a dramatic view of Delaware Bay, the North Atlantic Ocean, and the cape.

Delaware Art Museum, Wilmington
Visitors can explore a large collection of American art and the world's best permanent exhibit of Howard Pyle's paintings.

Delaware State House, Dover
The State House was the meeting place of Delaware's General Assembly until 1933. Tourists will see the Old State House, which has been restored to appear as it did in 1792, the year that the structure was completed.

Delaware Toy and Miniature Museum, Wilmington
Tourists can view more than 100 antique and modern dollhouses. Dolls, vases, and toys from the 1800s are also on display.

Fort Delaware, on Pea Patch Island, near Delaware City
Built in 1859, this former Union military fortress housed prisoners during the Civil War. Visitors can see people re-enact life at the time of the Civil War, and explore a museum.

Hagley Museum and Library, near Wilmington

The birthplace of the Du Pont Company, the Hagley Museum features a du Pont family mansion furnished in the style of the 1880s. Visitors can also tour Blacksmith Hill Worker's Community, powder yards, and a machine shop, all of which are restored to appear as they did in the 1800s.

Trap Pond State Park, near Laurel

Rent a canoe or a motorboat to explore this freshwater wetland, which features the northernmost bald cypress trees in the United States. In the past, wetlands extended over much of the nearby land.

Wilmington & Western Railroad, Wilmington

This railroad first began running in the 1870s. Modern tourists can enjoy a ride through the Red Clay Valley on old-fashioned trains.

Winterthur Museum, Garden, and Library

Henry Francis du Pont filled his family's 1838 mansion with American antiques and opened it to the public in 1951. Visitors can tour the large house and the 966-acre grounds, which include a garden just for kids, the Enchanted Woods.

Zwaanendael Museum, Lewes

This museum is home to artifacts from the *DeBraak*, a British navy ship that sank off the coast of Delaware in 1798. The wreck, discovered in 1984, has given researchers information about life at sea in the 1700s.

ANNUAL EVENTS

Georgetown Volunteer Fire Company's Annual Oyster Dinner, Georgetown—*February*

Great Delaware Kite Festival, Lewes—*April*

Old Dover Days, Dover—*May*

Point-to-Point Races, Winterthur—*May*

World Champion Weakfish Tournament, Milford—*May*

Wilmington Flower Market—*May*

St. Anthony's Italian Festival 5K, Wilmington—*June*

Delaware State Fair, Harrington—*July*

Watermelon Festival, Laurel—*August*

Brandywine Arts Festival, Wilmington—*September*

Nanticoke Indian Powwow, near Oak Orchard—*September*

Fall Harvest Festival and Quilt Show, Dover—*September*

Christmas and Candlelight Tours at Hagley Museum, Brandywine Valley—*December*

LEARN MORE ABOUT DELAWARE

BOOKS

General

Blashfield, Jean F. *Delaware.* New York: Children's Press, 2000.

Fradin, Dennis Brindell. *The Delaware Colony.* New York: Children's Press, 1992.

Fradin, Dennis Brindell, and Judith Bloom Fradin. *Delaware.* New York: Children's Press, 1996.

Whitehurst, Susan. *The Colony of Delaware.* New York: PowerKids Press, 2000.

Special Interest

Bierhorst, John, ed. *The White Deer and Other Stories Told by the Lenape.* New York: William Morrow & Company, 1995. A collection of traditional Lenape, or Delaware Indian, folktales and myths. For older readers.

Fiction

Heese, Karen. *A Light in the Storm: The Civil War Diary of Amelia Martin, Fenwick Island, Delaware, 1861.* New York: Scholastic, Inc., 1999. During the early 1860s, teenager Amelia helps her father tend a lighthouse off the coast of Delaware. She records in her diary her family's troubles, her adventures at the lighthouse, and how the Civil War divides Delaware.

Keehn, Sally M. *The Moon of Two Dark Horses.* New York: Philomel Books, 1995. Young Coshmoo, a Lenape Indian, and Daniel, a European settler, are unlikely friends. Their relationship is tested when the settlers and the Lenape go to war.

Laird, Marnie. *Water Rat.* New York: Winslow Press, 1998. Teenager Matt is cruelly nicknamed Water Rat because he's crippled and he loves to spend time exploring Delaware's rivers and bays. When he goes to stay with a local doctor, Matt uses his knowledge of the water to capture a band of pirates.

Pyle, Howard. *Bearskin.* New York: William Morrow & Company, 1997. This fairy tale by a Delaware author, first published in 1887, has updated illustrations. A young man who is raised by a bear learns that a princess is to be given to a three-headed dragon.

WEBSITES

Delaware.gov
<http://www.delaware.gov/>
Through its official website, Delaware's state government provides access to its services and offers information about the state.

Visit Delaware Home Page
<http://www.visitdelaware.net/>
The official site of the Delaware Tourism Office helps travelers learn about attractions, events, and accommodations in the first state.

The News Journal
<http://www.delawareonline.com/newsjournal/>
Stay up-to-date on the news from Delaware by reading Wilmington's daily newspaper.

Historical Society of Delaware—Grandma's Attic Kid's Museum
<http://www.hsd.org/kidsdiscvr.htm>
This site describes a historical exhibit about Delaware that's just for kids. Follow a link to learn more facts about Delaware's history, symbols, and famous women.

PRONUNCIATION GUIDE

Assawoman (AS-uh-wum-uhn)

Delaware (DEHL-uh-ware)

du Pont, Éleuthère Irénée (doo PAHNT, ay-luh-TARE ee-ray-NAY)

Lenape (luh-NAH-pay)

Nanticoke (NAN-tih-kohk)

Nemours (nuh-MOOR)

Newark (NOO-urk)

Piedmont (PEED-mahnt)

Rehoboth (rih-HOH-buhth)

Susquehannock (suhs-kwuh-HAN-uhk)

Sussex (SUHS-ihks)

Zwaanendael (SWAHN-uhn-dayl)

GLOSSARY

colony: a territory ruled by a country some distance away

constitution: the system of basic laws or rules of a government, society, or organization; the document in which these laws or rules are written

immigrant: a person who moves into a foreign country and settles there

Latino: a person living in the United States who either came from or has ancestors from Latin America. Latin America includes Mexico and most of Central and South America.

marsh: a spongy wetland soaked with water for long periods of time. Marshes are usually treeless. Grasses are the main form of vegetation.

nonpoint pollution: pollution coming from a widespread source rather than a specific point. Nonpoint sources of pollution include runoff from fields, pastures, and streets.

plantations: large estates, usually in a warm climate, on which crops are grown by workers who live on the estate. In the past, plantation owners usually used slave labor.

precipitation: rain, snow, sleet, hail, and other forms of moisture that fall to earth

runoff: water from rain, snow, or sprinklers that runs off the land and into streams, lakes, or the ocean. Runoff can carry pollutants from the air and the land.

swamp: a wetland permanently soaked with water. Woody plants (shrubs and trees) are the main form of vegetation.

turnpike: a highway on which a toll, or fee, is collected from drivers at various points along the route

urban: having to do with cities and large towns

INDEX

PHOTO ACKNOWLEDGMENTS

Cover (left): © William A. Bake/CORBIS; Cover (right): © Kevin Fleming/CORBIS; PresentationMaps, pp. 1, 8, 9, 50; © Scott T. Smith/CORBIS, p. 23; © Kevin Fleming/CORBIS, pp. 3, 36, 41, 45; © Gunter Marx Photography/CORBIS, pp. 4 (detail), 7 (detail), 17 (detail), 43 (detail), 53 (detail); © Kit Kittle/CORBIS, p. 6; Gene Ahrens, pp. 10, 11; Jerry Hennen, p. 12; © John Cunningham/Visuals Unlimited, pp. 14, 51; © Kitty Kohout/Root Resources, p. 15 (top right); John R. Patton, p. 15 (bottom left); William Sauts Netamuxwe Bock, p. 16; Library Company of Philidelphia, p. 19; John T. Kraft, Seton Hall University Museum, p. 20; © Bettmann/CORBIS, pp. 21, 35, 69 (2nd from top); Library of Congress, pp. 22, 32 (bottom); Permanent Collection of the University of Delaware, p. 23 (bottom left); Delaware State Archives, pp. 25, 27, 28, 38 (left), 39; Hagley Museum and Library, pp. 26, 33, 37, 38 (center and right); Historical Society of DE, pp. 29, 32 (top); Mae Scanlon, p. 30; © The Mariners Museum/CORBIS, p. 31; © CORBIS, pp. 34, 68 (bottom); Barbara Laatsch-Hupp/Laatsch-Hupp Photo, p. 42; © Walter Choroszewski, pp. 44, 46 (right); Winterthur, pp. 46 (left), 48; DE Development Office, p. 47; W. J. Talaroski/NE Stock Photo, pp. 49, 61; © Arthur Morris/Visuals Unlimited, p. 52; © Alan G. Nelson/Root Resources, p. 53; Marc Clery, p. 54; © W. A. Banaszewski/Visuals Unlimited, p. 55; © Doug Sokell/Visuals Unlimited, p. 56 (left); Bob Bowden, pp. 56 (right), 57 (left); Lynn Troy Maniscalco, p. 57 (right); Delmarva Poultry Industries, p. 58; Jim White, DE Nature Society, p. 59; George Karn, p. 60; Tim Seeley, pp. 63, 71, 72; Dictionary of American Portraits, pp. 66 (top and second from bottom), 67 (second from top and second from bottom), 68 (top); © Neal Preston/CORBIS, p. 66 (second from top); Yale Picture Collection, Manuscripts & Archives, Yale University Library, p. 66 (bottom); Du Pont, p. 67 (top); National Baseball Library & Archive, p. 67 (bottom); Deleware Art Museum, Howard Pyle Collection, p. 68 (second from top); Brown University Library, p. 68 (second from bottom); National Archives, p. 69 (top); Museum of Modern Art Film Stills Archive, p. 69 (second from bottom); Dallas Cowboys, p. 69 (bottom); Jean Matheny, p. 70; © Richard Day/Daybreak Imagery, p. 73.

DATE			